UP FROM THE PROJECTS

NOTEWORTHY AFRICAN AMERICANS WHO ONCE LIVED IN PUBLIC HOUSING

UP FROM THE PROJECTS

NOTEWORTHY AFRICAN AMERICANS WHO ONCE LIVED IN PUBLIC HOUSING

M A R Y   S O O D

AMESBURY PRESS, LOUISVILLE, KENTUCKY

Manufactured in the U.S.A.

IBSN 0-9630504-1-9

Library of Congress Card Catalog number 92-074197

Publisher: Amesbury Press, P.O. Box 22201,
Louisville, Kentucky 40252

Cover Photo: Mrs. U.S.A. 1991 Debra Williams,
Actor and producer Keenen Ivory Wayans,
and Ohio Congressman Louis Stokes.

DEDICATION

This book is dedicated to Anjali and Vinay for inspiring me to write, to my parents for their love and encouragement, to Michelle for hanging tough and graduating from Illinois State, to the late Mary Alice Blackmon and the late Rhonda Thompson, and to all the kids from LeClaire Courts--those who made it and those who didn't.

AUTHOR'S NOTE

A real estate developer, a producer with a hit television show, a university president, a congressman, a school superintendent, a medical doctor, a mayor, a principal, an author, a lawyer, a day care owner, a former Mrs. USA with a Ph.D....these are but a handful of the countless African Americans who have worked their way up from the public housing projects they once lived in.

A few of the individuals profiled in this book grew up with me in Chicago's LeClaire Courts. Others were strangers referred to me by organizations and agencies across the nation. Some are known nationally. Most are recognized primarily in their own communities. They are all noteworthy in that they have overcome the odds and made something of their lives.

I hope that their stories will sound an alarm for policy makers, educators, employers and anyone else who might be inclined to write off 'project kids'.

CONTENTS

Who would have guessed that these young brothers from the Outhwaite Homes public housing community in Cleveland would one day make history? Carl Stokes became the first Black mayor of a major American city. His older brother Louis is a member of the United States Congress.

Judge Carl Stokes, Cleveland Municipal Court
First Black mayor of a major American city

Former Cleveland Mayor Carl Stokes is a living legend. In addition
to being the first African-American mayor of a major city, he was
the first Black ever to be elected to all three branches of the
government, the legislative, the executive and the judicial.

Stokes, who is now a judge in the Cleveland Municipal Court,
didn't set out to make history. At 17 he dropped out of high
school to work in the steel mill, and admits that he might easily
have bypassed college and law school for a less impressive life as
a street hustler. Fortunately, a lifetime of conditioning by his
mother motivated him to follow in his older brother's footsteps and
pursue a higher education.

"My mother had fled from the south where she worked in the
fields, and wound up cleaning toilets in Cleveland instead of
working fields. Yet she had a unilateral optimism that if we got
an education things would turn out all right for us," Judge Stokes
reflects. "I don't know why she felt this way since nothing in her
lifetime of experience could have led her to this conclusion, but
she was right."

Judge Stokes' father died when he was only two years old.
Although there were a number of influential men who helped and
inspired him in later life, he had virtually no male role models in
his early years. But his mother's constant insistence that her
sons should get an education and make something of themselves made
up for the potentially damaging absence of a father figure.

After entering the military at age 18 and serving in the Army
of Occupation in Germany, Stokes returned to Cleveland to finish
high school. He then attended West Virginia State College and
Cleveland College of Western Reserve University. He went on to
earn a law degree from the University of Minnesota.

Before his mayoral election, Judge Stokes served as partner in
the law firm of Minor McCurdy, Stokes & Stokes. He became
assistant city prosecutor in 1958, and was the first African
American elected to the Ohio General Assembly in 1962. In 1967
Stokes attracted international attention when he was sworn in as
Mayor of Cleveland.

At times racism threatened to make his mayoral term untenable.
Whites who previously had sole access to lucrative city contracts
were alarmed and at times vengeful when Stokes insisted that
contracts be distributed equitably. Before Stokes' election there
was only one Black cabinet member. During his term, more than 270
African-Americans and other minorities were hired for or promoted
into supervisory or skilled city jobs.

8

Judge Stokes admits that racism was an obstacle, but believes that it is possible to beat racism. "There is no universal application of racism. It is not applied all the time in every instance, so you can beat it," Stokes says. "In the business of politics, if you can develop your own political base among your own people and have the ability to win a margin of support from those who are not blindly racist, you can win."

After two terms as mayor, Stokes declined to run again and worked on a local level, lecturing and doing political organizing in cities across the nation before joining WNBC-TV in New York, where he was the first Black anchor to appear daily on a television program in New York.

In 1980, after eight years as an award-winning broadcast journalist, Stokes returned to Cleveland to practice law and became the first Black lawyer to serve as general counsel to a major American labor union: the United Auto Workers. Stokes also represented Cleveland's largest city labor union.

In his autobiography, *Promises of Power* (Simon & Schuster, 1973), Judge Stokes wrote, "If I have been a lawyer, politician and TV anchor, I am still a kid from the public housing projects and never forget it."

Judge Stokes believes that the dismal state of today's projects will change only when the nation's leaders make public housing a priority. "Projects are all federally funded. In absence of a president who has concern about the multitudes of people in public housing, nothing is going to be done to change the condition of the projects. In absence of a president who is concerned, the state won't be concerned, cities won't be concerned."

Representative Louis Stokes, D-Ohio
United States Congress

The pipes at the Outhwaite Homes in Cleveland were so old that residents feared they would explode. It was a disaster waiting to happen. But Ohio Representative Louis Stokes helped save the day, and possibly a few lives, by securing a desperately needed ten million dollar renovation grant for the public housing community.

The irony of the whole situation is that Representative Stokes and his brother, Judge Carl Stokes, grew up at 4301 Case Court, right in the heart of the Outhwaite Homes.

"It's amazing to me that I'm in the position of representing the people in the projects where I grew up and, at the same time, representing the descendants of people who lived in the suburban homes where my mother had to scrub floors and wash clothes for eight dollars a day," marvels Stokes, who is one of the nation's most prominent African-American congressmen.

Representative Stokes gained international prominence in 1977 when he served as chairman of the House Select Committee on Assassinations, which investigated the assassinations of both John F. Kennedy and Martin Luther King, Jr. But Stokes has long been a hero to children in the projects of Cleveland.

A few years ago, when he spoke at East Tech, a high school near the public housing projects, a young man approached him after his presentation and said, "My brother and I live in the Outhwaite homes just like you and your brother did. We're going to do like you and your brother; we're going to be somebody."

Representative Stokes credits his mother for motivating him to succeed but laughingly confesses that she was very reserved in her praise. "If my kids pick up a pen off the floor, I tell them how great they are. But my mother didn't praise us much and I think to this day we continue trying to win her praise, trying to be seen in her eyes as having really done something special."

When Stokes graduated from high school, he joined the army so that he would be eligible for the GI Bill to further his education. He attended Case Western Reserve as an undergraduate, and earned his J.D. from Cleveland Marshall Law School in 1953. He practiced law for more than a dozen years, and was elected to Congress in 1968.

Outhwaite Homes has changed a great deal since the days when Representative Stokes and his brother Carl used to play basketball at the Portland-Outhwaite Recreation Center. "Everybody in the community used to be like one big family. We never saw the vacant, vandalized homes that exist there now. We never saw trash piled up outside the incinerators and lawns covered with weeds," he admits.

Although drugs and crime can make living in the projects more difficult than ever, overcoming the affects of racism and poverty has always been a challenge. "Many of the kids Carl and I grew up with are in jail or dead," Representative Stokes says. "At the same time, many of our friends were determined to overcome the odds and made something of themselves despite their humble upbringing. But it was easier back then. If we were growing up in the projects today, I don't know if we could have made it. I like to think that, with my mother's encouragement we could, but it would be far more difficult."

Debra Williams, Ph.D.
Clinical Psychologist
Former Mrs. U.S.A.

Dr. Debra Williams encountered considerable opposition when she decided to visit Chicago's Robert Taylor Homes during her reign as Mrs. USA 1991. Friends and associates warned the beautiful clinical psychologist that the projects might not be safe. Others suggested that housing project tenants wouldn't be able to appreciate or even relate to someone of her caliber. Despite these warnings, Williams went to the projects to speak.

When she stood before the crowd of Robert Taylor residents and announced that she had once lived in the nearby Robert Brooks projects, the tenant's roar of approval assured her that she had made the right choice.

"Visiting the projects turned out to be the most important thing I did during my entire reign. When they cheered me on I saw genuine hope in the faces of kids and adults. To them I was proof that you can come from the projects and go anywhere," says Williams, whose beauty has graced magazine covers and television commercials.

Before her reign as Mrs. USA, many recognized Williams only as the lovely wife of Dallas Maverick basketball star Herb Williams. But, although she puts her husband and their two children first, she has always had her own ambitions. In fact, she was already in graduate school when she first met her husband.

"I think it's important to be an individual in your own right. I have no problem with being Mrs. Herb Williams, but it feels good to know that I'm an accomplished professional. Herb respects that a lot," adds Williams.

Williams says she comes from a long line of strong, independent women and thanks her mother, her grandmother and other female relatives for teaching her to stand on her own two feet. She lived with her grandmother until she was in the third grade so that her divorced mother could go to nursing school. "My grandmother was very proud and very religious. She believed in church every Sunday and had me directing the choir at a small Baptist church in the middle of the projects," Williams recalls.

Williams left the projects after the third grade, when she went to live with her mother. Although statistics indicate that children raised in single-parent homes tend to fare worse in school and in life, Williams decided early on that she wasn't going to be a statistic.

In order to finance her college education, she began entering beauty pageants. She was second runner up in the Miss Black Teenager Pageant in 1977, and developed her poise and confidence as she went on to compete in other pageants.

Despite her celebrity status, Williams is surprisingly down to earth. In fact, she admits that she and her husband are far too practical to lead the excessive jet-setting lifestyle that some might expect them to live. "Both of us grew up poor. Herb can remember times when he didn't even have anything in the house to eat. We've never forgotten the value of a dollar. We're very conscious about what we're spending money on and we stay on a budget to take care of us down the stretch," Williams states.

Williams is often called upon to speak to young children and enjoys motivating them to succeed in life. "All children need to know that they have greatness inside. I want them to understand that they don't have to make excuses for not being great. They don't have to think that they can't be great because they don't have a daddy, or that they can't be great because they come from a bad neighborhood," Williams says, adding that successful African-Americans who grew up in the projects can be a real inspiration to children in the projects today. "If we can get over our fear of going back, we can use our expertise and our money to impact those communities instead of using all of it in communities that already have a lot of money and don't need us as much."

Who says jocks don't have brains? Former Baltimore Colts star running back Leonard Lyles made his mark on the playing field and in the business world.

Leonard E. Lyles, real estate developer

In Louisville, Kentucky prominent real estate developer Leonard Lyles is as well known for Lyles Mall and Lyles Plaza as he was once known for his exploits on the football field. The former Baltimore Colts star running back who was called 'the fastest man in football' in 1958, is now a star in the business world.

Seventeen years ago, Lyles developed Lyles Plaza, a strip shopping center housing six retail stores. In 1986 he pulled together a partnership to develop Lyles Mall, an impressive 70,000 square foot retail and office building which is the largest minority-owned retail development in Louisville.

Lyles is a former vice president of minority affairs for Batus, Inc., the U.S. holding and management company for the U.S. business interests of B.A.T. Industries. Prior to Batus, Lyles was employed at Brown & Williamson Tobacco Corporation, a subsidiary of Batus. He joined B&W in 1963 as a special sales representative during the summer months of his professional football career.

Lyles learned the work ethic early in life. His grandfather, who was a brick mason, taught Lyles how to build houses when he was only a teenager. Some summers Lyles would go to Tennessee to work on houses with his uncle. "I was always trying to make money. I knew that to make money you had to work," says Lyles.

Today the hard-working young man who grew up in Louisville's Shepherd Square housing project is one of the most prominent businessmen in Louisville. How did he do it?

"Discipline is the key," Lyles says without hesitation. "If you can't discipline yourself, you won't excel. Even if you have great talent, nine out of ten times you won't excel without discipline."

While many children are more interested in becoming football players than business leaders, Lyles is quick to turn them around when he speaks to boys in the community. "Anytime I talk to kids, I tell them that there's only a very small chance of becoming a professional athlete. I urge them to get an education, to get something between their ears. If they train to be president of the United States, that training will lend itself to other areas. If they only train to be athletes, they won't be able to do anything else."

Lyles frequently makes donations to youth recreation centers because he believes that these centers can keep children off the streets and give them something productive to do with their lives. Although he enjoys being in a position to give back to the community, Lyles is reluctant to advise other successful African American leaders about what they should be doing. "I hate to see African Americans fighting about who has or hasn't given back. I'm not going to impose my opinions on someone else," he says firmly.

Deborah Lewis, senior analyst
Soft Sheen Products, Inc

Working at a large Black-owned company has afforded Deborah Lewis opportunities that might otherwise have never come her way. As Soft Sheen's senior analyst she works closely with the vice president of planning and development, analyzing new products, ideas, goals and objectives and making sure the company is strategically positioned.

"At a Black company you get more of a chance for exposure. In white corporate America you are almost always limited. You seldom get to be on the inside. At Soft Sheen I've had an opportunity to be exposed to everything," states Lewis, who grew up in Chicago's Woodlawn public housing community.

Lewis was one of twelve children and the first one in the family to go to college. She sensed early on that she was different from her siblings and neighbors. "I didn't like the community I grew up in. I wanted more out of life. Going to college and having a career was just something that I wanted. I suppose some people can be inspired to want things, but it usually has to come from within, either you want it or you don't," says Lewis, who now owns a spacious Hyde Park condo and socializes with some of Chicago's most elite and successful. Her husband Charles owns Bodcharles, a maintenance and window washing company.

"I was always close to my mother, and seeing how she had so many children and was unable to fulfill her dreams convinced me not to put myself in that position," she says. Although Lewis always loved school, there was a time when she hated math. That changed when she entered the fifth grade. "One of my teachers really took time and worked with me. It gave me the desire to learn more and more."

Lewis earned a degree in Business Finance at Roosevelt University, where she joined Sigma Gamma Rho and established friendships with countless young Black women who came from similar backgrounds and had the same desire to improve their circumstances. She now represents her company in the Adopt-A-School program, and frequently gives motivational talks to high school students.

"Usually when kids ask me questions I can tell that they aren't serious. Sometimes only a few seem to be inspired, but if I can touch one child it's worth it," says Lewis. "I keep going because I would have liked for someone to have done this for me."

Lewis is leery of all the recent talk about revitalizing public housing, and is particularly critical of the tenant ownership plan. "Even if a tenant does buy a place in the projects, the chances of him being able to maintain it are slim. There would be some people in the community who worked and others who didn't. Some would try to keep their places up, others wouldn't."

"Changing public housing in Chicago is going to be a long process. What we need is to get people off of welfare because living on welfare can make people lazy. Keeping people on welfare is not helping anyone. We need to get people jobs, something that will make them feel good about themselves."

Adrienne Clarke, owner
Special Feelings Hair Salon

Starting your own business isn't always glamorous, even if you're in the business of making people look beautiful. Adrienne Clarke learned this lesson early on.

"I stumbled into hair because I was doing everyone's hair and it was fun and easy so I thought 'let me get paid for this'," says Clarke, who grew up in Chicago's LeClaire Courts public housing community.

Clarke trained at Pivot Point beauty school and, shortly thereafter, went to work for an upscale department store salon. Despite the salon's attractive interior and interesting clientele, Clarke was not content to remain there for more than a few years.

"In all honesty, I wanted to start my own business because of the money. They were taking such a large percentage of my pay at the place where I was working that I figured I'd do better on my own. Especially since I was doing all the work and they were taking all of the money," she admits.

While dreaming about her own shop was easy, turning those glamorous dreams into a reality was difficult. "I hadn't established credit so I couldn't lease furniture and equipment; I had to buy it. I worked in the department store's salon Wednesdays through Saturdays and on Mondays and Sundays I did hair in my mother's basement. I was so determined that I would have worked every day of the week if I had to. I saved all the money I made at home so that I could put it toward my business," Clarke recalls.

With her savings plus a loan from one of her brothers she pulled together the $16,000 she needed to start Special Feelings, which opened its doors in 1988 when she was only 25.

Clarke believes that the values she learned at home were what kept her striving to reach her dream. "We have 11 kids in the family and whatever we do we finish. We were never quitters. My older brother John, who is an electrician, recently started his own business. One of my sisters has been in college for over ten years. She went to college, got married, had two children and had to stop and start school many times, but she's about to graduate," Clarke says with pride. "I have a very supportive family. They told me when I started out that they would do whatever they could to help me. They bought little knickknacks for my shop and did a lot to inspire me. My parents always told me that no matter where you grow up, no matter who you are, you can do whatever you want. If you work hard, anything is possible."

Clarke frequently passes through LeClaire Courts and has nothing but fond memories of her thirteen years in the project. "I didn't want to move. I cried when we moved. All of my friends were there and generally the friends you grow up with are the ones you keep."

Edwin F. Bailey, Ph.D.
Dean of Student Development
St. Louis Community College, Meramec

Dr. Edwin Bailey has bittersweet memories of his childhood in St. Louis' infamous Pruitt Igoe Housing Projects. "We lived on the 10th floor and the elevator always seemed to be broken. Mother had asthma and it was difficult for her. Whenever we came home from shopping, mother would have to walk up a few flights of stairs then sit down and rest. We'd run upstairs with some of the bags then come back down and get more," recalls Bailey, who is Dean of Student Development at St. Louis Community College at Meramec.

Although Pruitt Igoe was nice and clean when Bailey's family first moved in, things deteriorated rapidly and maintenance slacked off. But no matter how dreary the environment became, there was a tremendous cooperation among the neighbors. "Mothers would come out and literally bleach the steps to get them as clean as possible. Families were strong knit and kids had to get sponges and help clean up the community," says Bailey.

In Bailey's home there was a strong emphasis on education. He was a bright child who skipped the fifth and seventh grade and graduated from elementary school at age 12. "My childhood was so positive that I can't remember any obstacles. My mother always encouraged us to read and I always had tremendous support from my parents and aunts and uncles," Bailey exclaims. "We used to make our own toys, and I remember finding scraps in the street and using them to build skate trucks. We didn't think that we were doing this because we couldn't afford real toys. We just felt that we were taking advantage of materials we found."

Whenever anyone expresses surprise that someone as successful as Bailey grew up in Pruitt Igoe, he quickly points out that he came from a strong family. "It's not where you live, but the kind of training and values you receive in a family unit," he states. "Outside of our community we were known as project kids, and most people were fearful of the projects. They heard all sorts of horror stories about what went on in Pruitt Igoe. But we were so involved in the church and scouting and other positive activities that we were never bothered by the stereotypes about us."

Bailey believes that growing up in public housing has helped him to appreciate the full range of existence in society, from poverty to life in suburbia. He attends a church located right in the heart of where Pruitt Igoe once stood, and is well-known and respected for his dedication to the African-American community. He is a Boy Scout leader and a member of a role model group that visits grammar schools and reads to children who seldom interact with Black professionals.

For almost twenty years Bailey served as director of financial aid for St. Louis Community College and spent a great deal of time visiting schools and churches and attending workshops where he encouraged high school children to go to college.

"My approach to the challenges that face us today is essentially one of rolling up ones' sleeves and working with the kids. We have to become involved on a personal basis, and we have to start with the very young. It's no longer good enough to write a check," Bailey says. "I am who I am because of the efforts of so many people--parents, teachers, church members. I know first hand how important support, encouragement and praise can be. I think it's my duty to do as much as I possibly can."

Bailey received a B.A. in Elementary Education at Harris Teachers College in 1965, and taught for seven years in St. Louis Public Elementary Schools. In 1972 he earned his M.Ed. in Guidance and Counseling at the University of Missouri. He earned a Ph.D. in Public Policy Analysis and Administration at St. Louis University in 1988. He and his wife Kathi have three children.

Sylvester Monroe, Time Magazine correspondent
Author, *Brothers* (Ballantine, 1989)

In the fall of 1986, Sylvester Monroe went back to the Robert Taylor Homes and the Prairie Courts, the two Chicago housing projects where he grew up. The Harvard-educated reporter returned to retrace his life and the lives of his closest childhood friends for a Newsweek Magazine series on African-American men. The award-winning story, co-authored by former Newsweek Senior Editor Peter Goldman, was later expanded into a best-selling book titled *Brothers*. Some critics considered it to be one of the most powerful books ever written on Black men in the inner city.

Growing up in the projects, Monroe constantly heard his Mississippi-born grandfather and uncles talking about the limitations placed on Black men. "They ain't gonna let a Black man do this or that. And if he gets too big, they'll kill him," the angry men often complained. While their words could easily have extinguished any flicker of hope in an impressionable boy, Monroe's optimistic mother gave him a more balanced perspective of what life could be like.

"My mother said that education was the key to the Black man's salvation in America. There are no guarantees in life, but without an education you can't even get into the ball game," says Monroe, who also credits the many unappreciated teachers in the Chicago public school system who encouraged him to excel.

Sylvester Monroe's life story reads like a classic Horatio Alger tale. At one moment he was a poor Black child living in the projects. Although he was a straight A student who loved to read F. Scott Fitzgerald and dreamed of one day writing a novel, at very best he was expected to go to a state college. And, undoubtedly, most people would probably consider that to be a major accomplishment for a youngster who grew up in public housing. But in Monroe's first year at Wendell Phillips public high school, he was awarded a scholarship to attend St. George's Preparatory School in Newport, Rhode Island. Suddenly expectations rose.

At St. George's he was one of only five Black students in a body of more than 200, and felt like a 'fish out of water' the moment he arrived. The majority of his classmates were from wealthy families who took for granted that their children would go on to Harvard. Students and faculty were quick to let Monroe know that, now that he was at St. George's, he had been elevated above 'common' negroes. Depressed, Monroe phoned his mother to see if he could go back to Chicago. "The only way you're coming home before you're supposed to is in a box," she replied, determined that her son would take advantage of this once-in-a-lifetime opportunity to attend such a prestigious school.

Monroe started an Afro-American student's association in his second year. He continued to excel in academics and, following the St. George's tradition, went on to Harvard where he majored in economics and American history. He earned his B.A. cum laude in 1973 and became a full-time correspondent at the Boston Bureau of Newsweek just three weeks after graduating. He studied at Stanford on a fellowship from the National Endowment for the Humanities from 1978 to 1980.

Reflecting on his experiences at these prestigious universities, Monroe states, "My greatest challenge was to get what these institutions had to offer and still maintain a Black identity; to get people to continue to see me as Black."

Monroe is now a Los Angeles correspondent for Time Magazine. "To write from a Black perspective and get that viewpoint reflected is difficult to do when you work for a mainstream magazine," he admits. But he continues to be a powerful voice for African-Americans, reporting on issues such as the Nation of Islam and its impact in the Black community. He covered Jesse Jackson's presidential campaigns in 1984 and 1988 and Harold Washington's election as mayor of Chicago in 1983. During his 15 years at Newsweek, he won several awards for his reporting on cover stories such as "Why Johnny Can't Write", "American Innovation" and "Why Public Schools are Flunking." Monroe has been with Time Magazine since 1989, and is a frequent public speaker at schools, colleges and conventions across the nation. He also contributed to the recently released book *Songs of My People* (Little, Brown and Co., 1992).

"Those of us who made it out of the projects have to make ourselves available as living, breathing role models who have been able to accomplish despite racism. That doesn't mean that we should go back and preach and talk down to people. We have to help them see beyond the probabilities; we have to show them the possibilities," states Monroe, who believes that many young people in public housing are crippled by poverty, racism, poor health, low self esteem and low expectations from teachers and practically everyone else.

Despite his enormous success, Monroe is reluctant to call himself lucky. "Luck is the intersection between preparation and opportunity," he says succinctly. He resides in Los Angeles with his wife Tonju Francois-Monroe and his son Jason. His daughter Sherita is a senior at Morris Brown College in Atlanta.

Dr. Rita Lewis
Third year resident, psychiatry
Rush Presbyterian St. Luke's Medical Center

When Dr. Rita Lewis talks about growing up in the projects in the sixties and seventies, you almost think she's describing an idyllic childhood in suburbia. Although her parents never went beyond high school, they had high standards and taught their children to appreciate the finer things in life.

The Lewis family lived in a corner apartment in Chicago's LeClaire Courts and had one of the largest, most beautiful lawns in the project. Every summer her mother's garden overflowed with fragrant pink roses. Her parents enjoyed opera music and kept quality art books in the living room. Her strict, Jamaican-born father demanded excellence in his children. While some neighborhood children could stay out most of the night and set their own rules, the Lewis children were expected to excel in academics, maintain a tidy household and be in the house early on school nights.

"On Sundays we had to clean the house. I remember washing dishes and listening to opera music. My parent's emphasis on education, hard work and discipline paid off because my sisters and brothers and I have all managed to be successful," laughs Dr. Lewis, who is a third year resident at Rush Presbyterian St. Luke's Hospital. "People hold doctors up as though we are out of reach. But all it takes to be a doctor is desire, self motivation and discipline. Naturally there are going to be obstacles. Sometimes there are mountains to climb, but we're all the better for having climbed them."

Dr. Lewis knows all about mountains. Although her excellent academic record helped her to earn impressive scholarships along the way, making it through Northwestern University was a great challenge. "My first semester at Northwestern, I was in shock. There were students strolling around campus in jeans and fur coats. It was so different from LeClaire Courts," she recalls.

When she became a single parent at the age of 22, a lot of people predicted that she would never be able to make it through medical school. But she was not one to be deterred by other people's negative attitudes.

"I saw so many of my friends give up their aspirations to become doctors. When I started in medical school there were twelve Black students in our class, only two of us finished. Some white college counselors would try to make us doubt ourselves. Instead of saying 'lets get a tutor' or 'you need to study harder', they would say that we might as well give up. This negative attitude can have a snowballing affect. It can make you doubt yourself, start making wrong moves and then start doubting yourself even more. But quitting never crossed my mind," says Dr. Lewis.

Dr. Lewis now lives in a home across the street from LeClaire Courts and is currently trying to pull together a group of former public housing residents to go back into the community and share their success stories with children in the projects. "Today things are worse than they were when I was growing up in the projects. Back then you'd see teenagers smoking marijuana or drinking alcohol on the corner. Now a lot of parents are on drugs and the kids are

raising themselves. But nothing is hopeless," Dr. Lewis believes.
"We have to reach kids in the projects and say 'Hey, I came from
the same conditions. Look what I've accomplished.' We have to let
them see that good things are not only available to the white man
and that while we might have to work twice as hard, we don't have
to assume that we can't have or achieve certain things just because
we're Black."

St. Philip's Principal Terry Flowers is pictured here in a moment
of relaxation. He is a determined headmaster whose students are
among the nation's brightest.

23

Terry Flowers, principal and executive director
St. Philip's School and Community Center, Dallas

St. Philip's School and Community Center is located in the heart of a community best known for its crack houses, prostitutes and winos. Many of the schools two hundred students come from low-income families. Yet, under the leadership of Headmaster Terry Flowers these students excel. Their test scores rank them among the top 13 percent in the nation.

Flowers was hired as St. Philip's assistant principal in 1983, when he was only 25 and already had three masters degrees under his belt. He is credited for turning around a school which was at that time dying a slow death due to financial woes. Faculty and parents call Flowers a miracle worker. Perhaps one key to Flower's success is that he knows first hand that almost any child can excel in academics, no matter how humble his or her background might be.

Flowers grew up in Chicago's Altgeld Gardens public housing community. There were plenty of bad influences in the community and they did not go unnoticed. "I remember seeing washers and dryers dropped over the rails in the high rises. Some people would throw bottles over the rails at pedestrians and police officers. I remember the smell of urine and the sense of danger, especially when the elevator was broken," Flowers says.

While working as a patrol boy at school, he was approached by gang members. "Fortunately, I had the ability to see negative role models and take them as an example of what I did not want to be like," says Flowers, whose mother taught him a 'trick' to avoid being recruited into a gang. "I learned that you don't tell your real age--you reduce it two or three years."

But Flowers does have some positive memories of life in public housing. "I had my family so I didn't need gangs. My brother and sisters all stuck together. My mother kept us in church and, for a long time, we feared my mother and then God. Eventually that turned around. There were a few positive role models in church. I had an uncle who drank but was still a positive influence in other ways."

While most men in the community weren't the kind of inspiring role models you read about in books or see on television, Flowers remembers that many of them would take time to talk to boys in the neighborhood and try to give them good advice.

When Flowers went to Upper Iowa University, where he would complete his bachelors in Elementary Education, he intended to become a teacher. He never considered that, as a principal, he could have an even greater impact on children.

"Ira Tolbert, my first Black instructor in college, told me 'You're active in the student union and your grades are good, you can teach or even become a principal'. Tolbert left me with a completely different goal; I was going to become a principal. I would not just get a B.A., but I would go to graduate school. He had elevated my aspirations. For the first time someone said that the sky was the limit," says Flowers, who has in turn elevated the aspirations and expectations of students and teachers at St. Philip's.

Flowers is currently pursuing a doctoral degree. He already has an M.A. in Early Childhood Education from the University of Northern Iowa and two masters in Education from Columbia University, one in curriculum, the other in administrative supervision. He reluctantly admits that few if any of the children he grew up with in the projects were able to break out of poverty and pursue their dreams.

Flowers and his wife Gernise have two daughters, ages four and six. The oldest attends St. Philip's, where her younger sister will join her as soon as she reaches school age.

Heager L. Hill, Deputy Manager
U.S. Department of Housing and Urban Development (HUD), Birmingham

Don't ask Heager Hill about the *projects*. He prefers the term public housing *community*. To Hill it isn't just a matter of semantics. "When people talk about the projects, it's always in a negative way," says Hill, who grew up in the Daniel Brooks public housing community in Hikes Point, North Carolina.

As Deputy Manager of HUD's Birmingham office, Hill assists in the overall administration of various HUD programs and FHA mortgage insurance programs. But, throughout his 22 years with HUD, he has been especially concerned about public housing residents. "I've always wanted to improve the lives of those in the lower income sector, and public housing is identified as the lowest rung of community life and living. Nothing gives me more pleasure than working in the area of urban development and seeing our programs help people. It's so rewarding to go into an area that has been uplifted," Hill says with enthusiasm. "There are drug elimination programs, sports initiatives to keep kids off the streets and, in some areas, tenant management programs that are working well."

He adds that there are also efforts underway to help tenant's develop entrepreneurial skills. In one community a tenant recently rented a truck and started a moving business.

Hill is convinced that individuals and organizations can make a difference in the lives of public housing residents. "At my 40th high school reunion all of my former classmates revered one man, the late Samuel Burford. He was our principal and he left a great impression on all of us," says Hill. "He took special interest in those of us who lived in public housing and made sure that we had what we needed. If we needed money, he gave money. If we needed transportation, he loaned us his car. And he did this in such a way that we never felt belittled. He even got me a scholarship to Morehouse."

Hill has devoted 30 years to government service. His first professional job was with the Redevelopment Commission of the City of Hikes Point. He has received numerous professional awards including HUD's Certificate of Merit Award presented by the Secretary; the United Negro College Fund Distinguished Volunteer Service Award; and the Distinguished Service Award of the Alabama Conference of Black Mayors. He and his wife Yvonne have two children.

Mayor Larry P. Langford
Fairfield, Alabama

Behind almost every successful man you'll find a mother who
motivated him with praise, encouragement, words of wisdom and
occasional threats.

Fairfield Alabama Mayor Larry Langford remembers many of his
mother's favorite mottos. "My mother used to say that 'If you can
get up one more time than you've been knocked down then you can be
successful.' She was a strong woman who had to hold together a
family of five children with absolutely nothing, and I was more
afraid of my mother than I was of the police," Langford admits.

When he was growing up in Loveman Village, a Birmingham
housing project, his mother urged him not to be a victim of his
circumstances. "A lot of people assumed that because we were from
the projects we had no future, that we'd probably end up in jail.
But mother told us that just because we were born in the projects
that didn't mean the projects were born in us," says Langford, who
is Fairfield's first Black mayor.

Langford's mother taught him and his five brothers and sisters
to cook, sew, clean and iron. He recalls washing pots that were
'bigger than myself' at a Birmingham restaurant where his mother
worked as a chef. By the time he was seven, he was earning money by
cutting grass. During his teen years he worked in an ice cream
shop. After graduating from high school in 1965, he joined the Air
Force so that he would be eligible for the GI Bill to further his
education. When his four years were up, he attended the University
of Alabama in Birmingham. In college he worked full-time.

Langford's first professional job was as a reporter at WBRC-TV
in Birmingham. In 1977 he won the Investigative Reporter of the
Year Award. Langford served on the Birmingham City Council from
1977 to 1979. Today Langford manages a city of 12,000, serves as
director of public relations for Budweiser Distributing Company and
hosts Hardline, a weekly radio program on WERC. He and his wife
Melva have one son. Despite Langford's myriad accomplishments, one
of the things he is most proud of is that he has never gone to
jail.

While many modest Southerners are reluctant to admit that they
grew up in the projects, Mayor Langford still goes back to visit
Loveman Village. "Anyone who is not from the projects doesn't
understand that there are great people who live in public housing.
But by the grace of God, some of the people who look down on public
housing tenants might end up there themselves. I'm not ashamed to

tell that I come out of the projects off of welfare."

As a child Langford used to pick up free cheese and other government surplus foods distributed by the Jefferson County Committee for Economic Opportunity. Ironically, he is now Chairman of the Board of Directors for the JCCEO and makes sure that people who receive surplus foods are treated with dignity and respect.

While society may construct countless roadblocks, Mayor Langford believes that kids from the projects can make it if they want to. Although today's projects are tougher than they were when he was a child, Mayor Langford believes that growing up in public housing isn't all bad. "I know children of doctors and lawyers who are in prison. Kids from the projects tend to be hungrier and succeed more than those who have everything given to them," says Langford. "At one point I had adopted the attitude that someone else was always responsible for my problems. It's easy to blame other people for your own shortcomings when you run into obstacles. But once you put God first, everything falls into place."

Dolores Cross, Ph.D., president
Chicago State University

In 1990, when Dr. Dolores Cross was named president of Chicago State University, she became the first Black woman to head a four year public university in Illinois. That was noteworthy. Two years later, when the struggling, primarily Black university reported a remarkable 40% increase in enrollment, that was front-page news.

But Chicago State's remarkable turn around came as no surprise to those who knew of Cross's impressive personal and professional accomplishments.

Although Cross married early and had two children by the age of 21, she was determined to get her college degree. She worked, raised her children and went to college simultaneously. It took her eight years to earn her Bachelors in Education at Seton Hall University. She went on to earn a master's from Hofstra University and a Ph.D. from the University of Michigan.

Her academic career began in 1961, when she worked as a special education teacher in New York city. She worked her way up into increasingly more challenging positions. In 1988, she became Associate Provost and Associate Vice President for Academic Affairs at the University of Minnesota. She has taught at Northwestern University and at Claremont and Brooklyn colleges; has been published in countless education journals; and has lectured on everything from developing leadership skills to equal access for women and minorities.

Last year, when she was in Newark, New Jersey for a speaking engagement, Cross jogged from her hotel downtown to Baxter Terrace, one of the housing projects she grew up in. "As I jogged around the entire complex, I was painfully aware of how different things were. I grew up in the early 1940's, a time when people thought things were going to get better. Now Baxter Terrace looks more like a correctional place than a housing project," Dr. Cross comments. "The city or state may be the worst landlord you'll ever get!"

Cross believes that many of the basic challenges of growing up in public housing have always been an issue. "In the projects you are aware of what's going on with the twelve or so other families in your building. You feel the impact of what's happening in those families, whether it's anxiety, unemployment or illness. You can't isolate yourself the way you can in suburbia so it does require more discipline to study and do other positive things given the distractions."

Many of Chicago State University's 8,000 students are single parents who live in public housing. Cross believes that her greatest challenge is to work with faculty, staff and administration to make sure that they improve student performance and help students to succeed. She teaches a Freshman seminar each semester to keep in touch with who her students are. Most of her students know that she is a marathon runner who believes that physical strength and good health make it easier to manage the demands of academia. She is a constant source of inspiration to students who, in some cases, never even dreamt that they would one day go to college.

"I know from experience that our students can succeed. There's no question in my mind that they can succeed. I know how many young people in the projects have potential," Cross says.

Karen Cervantes, site director
Girls Inc.

Karen Cervantes doesn't have sugar-coated memories of life in the projects. "I felt doomed," she admits, referring to her years in the West Dallas Housing Projects. "I thought I'd probably end up working at Burger King and have to settle for that. I thought I'd have to remain in the projects forever."

Luckily Cervantes' future turned out to be far brighter than she had anticipated. Although many of the children she grew up with succumbed to negative influences in the environment and are now strung out on drugs or perpetually unemployed, Cervantes has found a meaningful career as site director for the Oak Cliff region of Girls Inc.'s Dallas office.

Ironically it was Ruth Thomas, a Girls Inc. employee, who inspired Cervantes to do something positive with her life years ago. "I remember thinking 'I'd love to grow up and be like Ruth!' She counseled girls in the neighborhood and kept telling us that we didn't have to get pregnant, drop out of school and follow that pattern," Cervantes remembers.

But the route up and out of the projects was not an easy one. Cervantes' self esteem was badly damaged when she began being bused to a school outside of her community. "I remember being called nigger and made fun of. At one point, I hated being Black and hated being poor. I just thought 'Why are we poor? Why are we called niggers? Why can't we be one of the lucky ones?'"

At 17 Cervantes became pregnant by a young man she had fallen in love with and dated for three years. She was an honor student with scholarship offers, but college had to be postponed. She married her child's father and, a year later, they had another child. She and her husband Juan now have three children.

Cervantes has worked and gone to college part-time for eight years, and hopes to receive her B.A. soon. But the impact she has had on other young women in Dallas is far more valuable than any degree. She has helped countless girls steer clear of trouble and has counseled girls who have suffered from rape and other traumatic experiences. At times she worries about 'crossing the line' and getting too involved in the girl's personal lives, but that doesn't stop her from going miles beyond the call of duty.

In 1989 Cervantes was flown to Washington where she received a Congressional Medal for her volunteer leadership skills. More recently she received national recognition for her role in 'Literacy is it me?' a Girls Inc. program to promote literacy.

"Somebody needs to just hand my degree over, 'cause I've earned it," laughs Cervantes.

Unlike many older individuals who remember the good old days when the projects were friendly and well-maintained, Cervantes is only 25 and has a far less romantic view of public housing. "I can't think of any advantage to growing up in the projects, except that you can look back and tell others that you made it out and so can they."

Berlaind Brashear, attorney-at-law
Former Judge, Dallas County Criminal Courts

In 1977 Judge Berlaind Brashear became the first African American judge in the Dallas County Criminal Courts. Although racism had prevented him from landing a job as a prosecutor when he finished Thurgood Marshall Law School, racism was not his greatest obstacle in life.

"Learning to accept my own Blackness was my biggest obstacle. A lot of Black people don't want to admit it, but learning to accept ourselves can be hard. Back when I was growing up, Black was ugly even to Black folks. Other kids would tease me because of my very dark skin and African features," says Brashear, who grew up in the Frazier Court projects in Dallas in the 1940's. "Eventually it dawned on me that I had to develop a sense of humor and not be so sensitive about my color. It was hard to do, but I slowly learned that Black wasn't ugly--that God created me this way and I was not inferior."

Brashear never felt that growing up in the projects was detrimental in any way. "Back then everyone was poor so there was no stigma attached to living in the projects. Everyone in my community believed in hard work and taking care of one's family. Parents didn't tolerate stealing. Good values were taught in almost everyone's home," says Brashear.

When he was seven years old, Brashear met Pearl Harbor war hero Dori Miller and, for many years after that, Brashear dreamed of one day becoming a sailor. But he was drawn to a law career because of the gross injustices he witnessed as a teenager. "I saw people commit murder and get away with it because nobody would enforce the law as long as the victim was Black. Back then you could go out and kill a Black person and if you had five hundred dollars you could be out of jail the next day," says Brashear. "They didn't even hire Black prosecutors back in those days. When I went to apply for a job as a prosecutor, they laughed me out of the office." But Brashear had the last laugh; he eventually became one of the most prominent and respected judges in Dallas.

Ever so often, Judge Brashear likes to go back to Frazier Courts. "I like to look around and talk to folks, and try to figure out where our house was. I take a great deal of pride in coming from there."

Melvin Bradley
Garth & Bradley, public relations

Melvin Bradley isn't one to rest on his laurels. Bradley, who served as former President Ronald Reagan's special assistant for policy development and now runs his own Washington, D.C.-based public relations firm, says he still doesn't view himself as a 'great success'.

"I'm just a country boy from Texarkana, Texas who has had to work hard for everything he has attained. I'm still searching for that which is better. My notion that there is always something better helped me to push forward when I was in the projects, and I'm still pushing," says Bradley, whose clientele includes major fortune 500 companies and some smaller minority-owned firms.

Bradley developed a strong work ethic early in life by doing odd jobs like helping neighbors to paint and delivering packages. His first 'real' job was at a grocery store where he stocked canned goods. He sensed that there had to be something better than his life in the Steven's Court housing project where he lived, and decided to figure out a strategy to help him move up and out. Someone told him that the key to success was staying in school, working hard, and respecting ones' neighbors and parents. "I dismissed this as advice from old people," Bradley admits, but he soon figured out that it was the best route to take.

Although Bradley is quick to admit that he doesn't know the answer to the problems facing young people growing up in housing projects today, he suspects that public housing tenants would be more confident if they realized that they were well-equipped to compete with others.

"In the projects you watch TV and read about congressmen and secretaries and the likes, and you are in awe. But one thing I learned when I came to Washington D.C. is that all the brains are not in the capitol. A lot of brains are in the projects. I learned that I could play with the big boys," says Bradley. "Kids from the projects need to learn that even though they may have gone to the neighborhood school, they are just as good or better than the Ivy League boys. Once they meet and have lunch with an Ivy Leaguer they will realize that he is not the self-confident, brilliant, all-powerful person they might have thought that he was. Going to Harvard doesn't make someone brighter or better. If you work hard and prepare yourself you can go eyeball to eyeball with anyone."

Bradley dreamt of starting his own business for many years. "Years ago I helped a friend start an auto dealership. Although I wasn't the main actor in that business, I gained a great deal of experience from that. I wanted to start my own business because I wanted to control my own destiny," Bradley states. But he and Ruth, his wife of 32 years, had four children to raise. It wasn't until Bradley's children grew up that he was in a position to start his own firm.

Bradley urges children to keep their eyes on the prize. "Stay focused on your goals and remember there is a better life out there. Stay in school, work hard and avenues will open up to you."

Harold Jerome Jackson, editorial writer
Birmingham News

In Birmingham, Alabama it's no secret that many of the city's most dynamic citizens once lived in public housing. Pulitzer prize winning Birmingham News editorial writer Harold Jerome Jackson, who has been earning impressive awards and accolades for over two decades, is one of Birmingham's many high-profile leaders who grew up in the Loveman Village housing project.

Jackson, who joined the Birmingham News in 1986, brought to the paper a sensitivity which the media is in desperate need of. When a poorly managed Public Housing Authority became headline news in Birmingham, project tenants were fortunate to have an editorial writer with Jackson's background working at the state's largest newspaper. "It was important for me to make sure we didn't portray housing project tenants as somehow less than full citizens, as someone the rest of the city should not care about," says Jackson, who was the National Association of Black Journalists Journalist of the Year in 1991. "There are still a lot of good families in the projects, families who help their children to excel. Too often their stories don't get told."

When a local television station did a five-minute profile on Jackson, he had an opportunity to walk through Loveman Village and interact with current residents. "I talked to six kids and they told me they wanted to go to college and be achievers. I asked if they knew that it would require hard work, and they said that they were prepared for that."

Jackson was born in 1953, before the projects became a dangerous place to live. But by the time he graduated from college he did witness shootings and stabbings. "I had many opportunities to decide that I didn't want to go the academic route. But my parents were strict and I didn't spend a lot of time in the streets," says Jackson, who was a bookworm and high achiever even as a child.

In addition to winning a Pulitzer in 1991, Jackson has won three Hector Awards, Sigma Delta Chi's Green Eyeshade Award, the UPI Feature Writing Prize and the Associated Press News Writing Award.

At a time when society is so focused on the plight of African American men, it is refreshing to know that Jackson and his four brothers all went to college and established successful careers. Jackson is dedicated to doing volunteer work that allows him to give back to the community. He visits schools where he reads stories to kindergarten kids from the projects and tells them about his job. While Jackson encourages all former project residents to try to give back to the community, he warns that successful African Americans should not feel guilty about their own achievements. "Sometimes guilt forces us to do things, but in too many cases guilt is a hinderance. Some people feel guilty to the point where they divorce themselves from their past. They feel as though they can't possibly do enough, so they do nothing."

Jackson and his wife Denice Estell Pledger have two children.

Linda Maxwell, senior associate
Coopers & Lybrand

Linda Maxwell would like to go home. But like so many African-Americans who are climbing the sometimes wobbly corporate ladder, she doesn't have a lot of spare time. Her position as a senior associate at Coopers & Lybrand is demanding and competitive. And even if she did have time to go back to the projects, there is another very real issue that she has to grapple with--safety.

"I grew up in the Cypress Hills projects in Brooklyn and I've heard that it's a war zone," Maxwell admits. "It would be nice to be able to go back regularly to speak to young teens there because it's so hard for them to be motivated when there is no one around to encourage them. But I admit that I am concerned about safety. If something happened to me, where would my family be?"

Maxwell's concerns are familiar to many successful Blacks, but she never uses fear as an excuse to do nothing. Instead, she serves as a mentor to countless young Black professionals. "Many young Blacks aren't fully aware of racism and how to work around it. They'll confess their lack of experience, for example, and not realize that this may give employers the excuse they were looking for to say 'I'm sorry but you're not ready to be promoted'."

Maxwell and her two sisters were groomed for success at an early age. She fondly recalls how her Jamaican-born father used to take the family up to Harlem to see African art exhibits. He had attended Marcus Garvey rallies in his younger days and made sure that his daughters were politically aware. Unfortunately, he had only a third grade education and could not help his daughters with science, math and other important subjects. It was Maxwell's mother who was most concerned about her daughters' formal education and adamant about them going to college.

"My mother was determined that our life would be better than hers was, and that we would have the opportunities she didn't have. She had wanted to go to college desperately. Her father tried to get a loan for her schooling but the bank said they would give him money for seeds but they wouldn't give him money to send his daughter to college," says Maxwell, who earned a Bachelors in Nursing at the University of Connecticut, a Masters in Nursing at the University of Pittsburgh, a computer training certificate at DePaul and thirty credits in National Information Systems at California State University. Her older sister is an assistant instructor in English at North Carolina State University. Her younger sister is a manager at Ernst & Young.

The highest point in Maxwell's academic life was when she passed the nursing board examination on her first try. "I knew that getting through the science section would be a major obstacle, but I studied three times as hard as most people study, and ended up scoring very high in the sciences."

While her fast-paced career often keeps her on the road, she keeps her feet on the ground and never forgets where she came from. "I remember seeing Jim Crow signs and seeing teachers accuse Black children of cheating when they scored high. But growing up in the projects gave me the ability to succeed no matter what."

Joseph James, chief counsel
U. S. Department of Housing and Urban Development (HUD)-Kansas City

One of Joseph James' favorite childhood hangouts was the public library. He was a studious child who enjoyed the pursuit of knowledge. But just getting to the library adjacent to the Pruitt Igoe projects in St. Louis was sometimes risky, and being a good kid didn't guarantee his safety.

"I remember having my books ripped apart and thrown in the snow," says James, who is now Chief Counsel at HUD's Regional Office in Kansas City. "There were kids who would literally try to force other kids to do drugs so that they'd be like them."

The best social workers and psychologists in America can't explain exactly why some kids make it out of the ghetto and others don't, but James pinpoints two factors that helped him move forward. One was the public library, where he would sit for hours reading about Thurgood Marshall in Ebony and other publications. The other was his mother, who taught Christian values and insisted that her children do their best in school.

"We were never taught hatred, dislike and bitterness. Anybody who starts with bitterness can't be successful. You can't hold grudges just because you're less fortunate than others, and go around blaming other people who have nothing to do with your misfortune," says James.

James' mother also insisted that her sons join the Boy Scouts. Scouting had such a positive impact on James' life that he is now an assistant pack leader.

Although there were many good families in Pruitt Igoe, James discovered early on that project tenants were looked down on by others. "A lot of people associated the worst of Pruitt Igoe with everyone in the community. They assumed that we had no values and wanted nothing out of life. Many teachers today have this attitude about kids from the projects, so if grooming is a problem or if clothes are a problem it's easy for kids to say 'I'm not going to school...I'll just get a survival job.' It's easy to give up if society expects nothing of you," says James, who graduated from law school at Texas Southern University.

Years ago, during a stint as a YMCA counselor, he went back to the projects to counsel children in the community. "One of the biggest problems in housing projects is that there is no viable support system. Those of us who grew up in the projects have to keep trying to go back and help because people who aren't sensitive to the challenges facing public housing tenants won't do it. No matter how turned off the beneficiaries of our help may seem to be, we have to keep trying."

Zan Holmes, Jr., Pastor
St. Luke's Community United Methodist Church

Ask Dallasites to name the most dynamic church in town and they'll probably say St. Luke's Community United Methodist, where Sunday worshippers have to arrive fifteen minutes early just to get a seat at the *back* of the church.

Under the leadership of Pastor Zan Holmes, who once lived in the Roseland Homes projects in Dallas, St. Luke's has been at the forefront of social, economic and political change. "God didn't bless us for nothin'," the Pastor likes to tell his congregation of 3,000. "God blesses us so that we can be a blessing to others. We seek healing from God so that we can be instruments of healing in others."

St. Luke's instruments of healing are present throughout the city. The church has over 75 ministries, including an economic development ministry, an employment ministry, a jail ministry and a teen parent ministry.

Pastor Holmes calls himself an 'unabashedly African-American minister', and often preaches from an Afrocentric perspective. One of the first things St. Luke's visitors notice is a beautiful stained glass image of a Black Christ. On religious holidays Holmes urges members to wear African garments purchased from African and African-American vendors. The church publishes a directory of Black businesses and has a telephone line which job seekers can phone to find out about employment opportunities in Dallas and elsewhere.

Although St. Luke's congregation includes many prominent and well-educated Dallasites, Pastor Holmes is focused on the plight of the disenfranchised and impoverished. He believes that much of the crime in housing projects and other poor communities is a direct result of a system which blames the impoverished victim while ignoring the wealthy perpetrators. "Think! We have to think," he exclaims. "If we were thinking we wouldn't be asking why there are drugs in the streets, we'd be asking why there are drugs in the suites."

Pastor Holmes influence is not limited to Dallas. As an adjunct professor at Southern Methodist University's Perkin's School of Theology he has trained ministers who have in turn created progressive churches throughout the nation and overseas. Pastor Holmes served in the Texas legislature from 1960 to 1972. He has served on the Board of Directors for countless organizations and received numerous prestigious awards including the 1990

Peacemaker Award and the 1991 Living Legend Award.

He holds a B.A. from Houston-Tillotson College, a Bachelor of Divinity and a Master of Sacred Theology from Southern Methodist University, and an honorary Doctor of Divinity from Houston-Tillotson College.

In 1991, African-Americans who were fed up with political exclusion and racist city policies almost convinced the popular pastor to run for mayor of Dallas. More recently he was urged to become a Bishop. He turned down both opportunities due to his commitment to St. Luke's.

Pastor Holmes grew up in the Black church, where he was constantly exposed to positive African American role models. He urges young men in the projects to get involved with the church, the YMCA and other organized groups. He also encourages more affluent African Americans to make their presence known in the projects.

Darryl T. Owens, county commissioner
Jefferson County, Kentucky

When his daughters were young, County Commissioner Darryl Owens liked to drive through the Shepherd Square housing project in Louisville to show them where he grew up.

"They'd say 'Oh, here we go again' whenever I headed toward the projects," Owens laughs, but he felt that it was vital for his daughters to learn not to pre-judge people because they were poor and from the projects.

"When I was growing up in the 1950s, many of us were in the same economic situation but we all had pride because we were poor without anyone calling us poor. The problem today is that we categorize everyone. I think that gives you the idea that because you come from the projects the level of expectation is lower. This happened to some extent when I was in school, but today it's magnified because there is a much more negative view of the projects," says Owens.

As a child Owens always slept on a sofa or hide-away bed in the living room because his family's apartment had only one bedroom, which was shared by his mother and sister. Although he had no father figure in the home, his uncle was a good role model and a number of fathers in the community showed by example how responsible men were supposed to behave.

"When people think of the projects they think of men who drink, beat their wives and curse a lot. But we had some responsible hard-working men in the community who made an impression on us even though we didn't know it at the time," says Owens.

Owens' mother was no slouch when it came to disciplining her children. "On Saturdays I didn't leave to go *no* place until I cleaned the cement steps and got the knife to get in the corners," he recalls. "One of the things that kept us on the straight and narrow was fear of our parents. If you even looked like you were thinking something wrong, you could pick yourself off the floor."

When Owens was a teenager, he and a group of his friends stole soda bottles from a parked delivery truck. "After I stole them I knew I couldn't bring them home. But today kids are walking home with stolen televisions and VCRs and nobody asks anything."

When Owens finished high school he wanted to enter the Navy but, at his mother's urging, agreed to attend college for one year. As his mother had hoped, he stayed in college and ended up graduating from Central State in Wilberforce, Ohio and going on to

Howard Law School.

In 1983 Owens was elected county commissioner of Jefferson County, the most populous county in Kentucky. He has sponsored legislation such as collective bargaining for public employees, a landlord tenant ordinance and a minority vendors contract. He has served the Louisville community as a civic leader in a broad range of organizations. A recent local newspaper poll indicated that he was among the city's most respected African American leaders.

At times Owens finds it difficult to have an impact on children today. He sometimes encounters teens who automatically assume that he knows nothing about being poor. "If you appear to be successful, some children can't relate to you," he acknowledges. But that hasn't stopped him from reaching out.

Owens tries to avoid giving teenagers cliche pep talks about working hard and staying out of trouble. Instead, he tries to give them practical advice, encouraging teens to "look teachers straight in the eye," for example.

"If you look people in the eye it gives you a certain confidence. It gives people a certain respect for you if you can talk eyeball to eyeball as opposed to eyeball to top of the head," says Owens, who believes it is easier for teachers to dismiss and categorize students who lack confidence.

Recently, when a group of Louisville students were asked what they wanted to be when they grew up, many said they wanted to be like Michael Jackson and other celebrities. But, much to Owens' surprise, one student responded 'I want to be like Commissioner Owens.'

Mae Beck
Day Care Owner and Activist

From the time she was in the seventh grade, Dallas day care owner Mae Beck used to go with her mother to clean white people's homes.

"Through no fault of her own, my mother just assumed that I would be a domestic worker. Like many of our parents, she couldn't see that a better day was coming because she had never seen a better day," says Beck.

"When I was about 16, I started going to white people's homes to work by myself. When I got to one woman's home she had a particularly dirty task for me. She wanted me to clean a very large old oven. I had worn my uniform to work so I didn't have changing clothes. I asked her for an apron or an old rag to wear. She refused to give me one. So after cleaning the oven, I had to go home on the bus filthy from my neck to my toes. I remember thinking that white people must enjoy seeing us in these kind of slave-like roles."

But this experience didn't make Beck bitter; it made her determined to never have to rely on white people for a living. Inspired by a successful neighbor who owned her own beauty shop, Beck was determined to work her way out of the Frazier Court projects where she grew up and make something of herself. After work she would come home and watch civil rights marchers on television and dream of one day going to college and having a better life. But financing her education was a major obstacle.

"My mother was divorced with six children. We all grew up on welfare. I knew that the only way I could go to college was if I sent myself, and that's what I did," says Beck, who had been prepared for this struggle by the many inspiring teachers she had in elementary school and in high school. "I had attended all-Black schools where the teachers really cared about us and told us repeatedly that we would have to be better than whites if we wanted to be able to compete with them."

To finance her education at Bishop College, Beck worked from four o'clock in the afternoon until one o'clock in the morning at Texas Instruments. "A lot of people at Texas Instruments didn't have cars so I had to pick up and drop off five riders every night. That meant not getting home until two in the morning, and studying from two until four a.m. every day," Beck says.

Juggling a full load of college credits and working full-time proved to be overwhelming and Beck dropped out of college in her junior year. It took seventeen years for her to return to college and earn a B.A. at Dallas Baptist University, but those seventeen years in between were productive. Inspired by her grandfather, who was a minister and owned rental property, she began investing in real estate at the age of twenty-five. When she met and married prominent Dallas artist Arthello Beck, they saved money and purchased more real estate.

In 1978 she opened Saner Avenue Children's Center. "I decided to start my own business when I saw whites with less education being moved up before me at work. I opened a day care center because I wanted to be with my younger child, and because I saw a need for good child care in the African American community."

Beck formed the Black Coalition of Concerned Citizens for Child Care because she felt that state funds for child care were going primarily to white child care facilities, forcing Black parents to take their children outside of the community for day care. With the help of African American political leaders, Beck saw to it that changes were made. "Now state-funded children can go to any child care center their parent's choose," says Beck.

In retrospect, Beck believes that she might never have been so successful had she not grown up in the projects. "The only reason I worked so hard to get an education and make a decent living was because I didn't want to stay in the projects. I wanted my house to be as nice or nicer than the white folks' homes I worked in."

Dr. Charles Goosby, Dentist

Prominent Atlanta dentist Charles Goosby doesn't expect to be praised for working his way out of the University Homes Housing Projects. "Things used to be so much easier than they are today. You wouldn't believe how inexpensive college tuition was when I was in school. In those days you could work over the summer and make enough money to cover your entire tuition," says Goosby, who graduated from Morehouse and MeHarry. "My mother worked as a domestic earning eight dollars a week and she was able to get up enough money for me to study. It's far more difficult to finance a medical education today. The cost is so staggering that students are often very deeply in debt by the time they graduate."

"There weren't as many temptations back then as there are today either. You certainly didn't have the drug scene you have today. We lived in University Homes during a time period in which moving into the projects meant going from an icebox to a refrigerator, from a wood stove to a gas stove, from a back porch bathroom to one with running water. It meant having a radiator for heat instead of a stove for heat," recalls Goosby, who is a volunteer for the Boy Scouts of America and an active member of St. Paul of the Cross Church.

As a child, Goosby was surrounded by individuals who encouraged him to excel in school and kept him from going in the wrong direction. "If someone gave me a pat on the back, I'd jump through hoops for them. My teachers, parents and other family members knew this so they gave me a lot of praise. I didn't want to be caught doing anything wrong by anybody in the neighborhood because they were privy to whooping my behind and then sending me home where I'd be whooped again."

After making toothpaste powder in a high school science class Goosby decided to become a dentist. A close family friend who happened to be a dentist provided encouragement and some financial assistance.

Goosby believes that teens growing up in public housing today have to be more disciplined than ever if they hope to make it through medical school. "They've got to be in control of their lives and do that which needs to be done in order to accomplish their goals. If that means staying up late to study, they have to do that. If it means not going out on dates, they have to forego dating. They have to keep their eyes on the prize and do all the things that are going to help them accomplish their goals."

43

Calvin W. Rolark
Publisher, Washington Informer
Founder, United Black Fund of America

In the late 1960s, a Black Baptist minister in charge of a senior citizens' home reportedly asked the United Givers Fund for $10,000 dollars. He was turned down. In the same year, the United Givers Fund reportedly granted $200,000 dollars to a white charity which happened to be located in one of the nation's wealthiest counties.

Washington D.C. newspaper publisher Calvin Rolark took this case as a sign that African Americans could not rely on outsiders to fund Black social service agencies, programs and causes. "It dawned on me that in as much as there are Jewish, WASP and, in some areas, Ku Klux Klan funds, we needed a Black fund," says Rolark.

He had already founded the Washington Informer, a Black weekly newspaper which now boasts an impressive circulation of 27,000 in and around the nation's capitol. When he set out to create the United Black Fund of America in 1969, he had no idea that it would one day become a nationally prominent, multi-million dollar organization. But the United Black Fund grew into a network of non-profit agencies that provide human care services to low-income and disabled African Americans and other minorities. The Fund assists the disadvantaged in being self sufficient by providing funding to member agencies for the establishment of diverse health and welfare programs.

"The only people who can save us is us," says Rolark, who grew up in the Steven's Court public housing community in Texarkana, Texas.

Rolark believes that integration, which led working-class and middle-class African Americans out of Black communities, is largely to blame for the dismal state of public housing today. "Black people haven't learned what other people have learned; other races like to stay together. I enjoy being around other Black people," says Rolark. "When I was growing up in the projects, we felt that we had achieved something to be living in public housing. There were flowers in the lawns and a friendly atmosphere. We had a recreation center, a football field and tennis courts. We could leave our doors open at night."

There were no shortage of excellent role models in the community where Rolark's family resided. "We were poor, but everybody worked. My father was a mechanic and my mother later opened Rolark's Snack Shack. Some of our teachers lived in the community, and kids were competitive grade-wise," says Rolark. "One of our teachers became a manager in the project and talked to my brother and me about going to Prairieview College."

Rolark finished high school when he was only 15 and graduated from Prairieview at 19. He went on to Michigan State University and to Cornell.

When asked if he was ever concerned about the stigma of being a product of public housing, Rolark quickly responds, "Once you know who you are, you don't worry about stigmas!"

Shirley Martin (r) of Tidy Team Janitorial Services in Chicago is pictured with business partner Renee Bailey. In the photo below are Martin's parents Annie Mae and Willie L. King as they appeared when they moved into LeClaire Courts, where they have lived for 36 years. To help Martin launch her business, her parents helped clean her client's offices, baby-sat her daughter and inspired her to keep going when she was almost prepared to give up.

Shirley Martin, owner
Tidy Team Janitorial Services
Support systems specialist, Rush Presbyterian St. Luke's

Shirley Martin never imagined that she would one day own Tidy Team, a Chicago-based janitorial service.

"When I was growing up in the projects, I never gave a great deal of thought to what I would do with my future. I always had secretarial jobs in high school because I liked earning money for clothes. But I never really thought about having a career, and I certainly never contemplated starting my own business," admits Martin.

It was almost by sheer coincidence that Martin even went to college. "I was at a friend's house one Saturday and her sisters were helping her to fill out financial aid forms for Illinois State University. I decided to fill out one too."

Although Martin's parent's struggled to send her to a Catholic grammar school and encouraged her moral development, they didn't have the background and experience to help her choose a major or otherwise plan her college career.

Illinois State University turned out to be 'one big party' for Martin. "I wasn't a serious student. I didn't have my priorities straight and no one sat me down and told me how important college was. Almost all of my friends dropped out by the end of our freshman year."

Martin transferred to Kentucky State University to get a fresh start and sever her ties with friends who weren't serious about school. She made the honor roll at Kentucky State but the financial strain of going to an out-of-state college was too great. She dropped out in her Junior year to take a secretarial job in Chicago.

She took numerous college courses over the years but found that there were always new obstacles. School was even more costly than before because she had a full-time job and was no longer eligible for financial aid. She slowly worked her way out of the secretarial pool but always had regrets about not finishing college.

"After I got married and had a child, I felt determined to turn my life around immediately. I wanted my daughter to have a home and all of the advantages I never had, so I actually started working two full-time secretarial jobs. There were professionals out there earning more in 40 hours than I was earning in 80," Martin says. Eventually she quit her night job because she knew that her daughter needed more attention, but her desire to move ahead did not subside.

She continued taking college-level computer courses and various self-improvement classes and, after several promotions, became a systems support specialist at Rush Presbyterian St. Luke's hospital. Over the years she and her best friend, Renee Bailey, talked a great deal about starting their own business. Finally they decided to stop procrastinating and, last year, they started Tidy Team. Working full-time and running a cleaning business is often challenging, but Martin is determined to succeed.

"I think it's important for me to do well because I can't demand that my daughter study and work hard in school if I'm not also trying to accomplish things in my life. One of the best things about having my own business is that my daughter is learning the value of being an entrepreneur," says Martin, who is an active member of the School Improvement Plan Committee at her child's grammar school.

"It took me about a dozen years to work my way up to a level which I could have reached years ago had I only stayed in school. My strongest advice to any young people in the projects today is that they go to college and don't leave until they have at least one degree in hand."

Martin and her husband George recently purchased their first home. "This is a big deal in that I am the first one in my immediate family to ever buy a home," says Martin, whose parents and younger brother still reside in the LeClaire Courts housing project where she grew up.

Wesley L. Campbell, associate pastor
Star of Hope Church
Manager of Continuing Education, Tyler Junior College

When Wesley Campbell earned a B.A. in electrical engineering at Purdue it was a victory for his entire family.

"My older sisters used to work with me on math problems, and they always said that I was going to college," says Campbell, who comes from a close-knit and loving family.

Although Campbell seemed destined for a math-related career, a teacher he had met at Purdue inspired him to eventually pursue a masters in Biblical Studies at Dallas Theological Seminary. "This teacher was a minister, and seeing how he lived his life made me want to be a minister. One time he read an article in the newspaper about a man who had been put in prison unjustly. He immediately got on the telephone and reached out to help this man even though he was a complete stranger," says Campbell, who grew up in the Ida B. Wells and Robert Taylor projects in Chicago.

Campbell is now pursuing an M.S. in math at the University of Texas, but he eventually plans to open an urban church and school to minister to African Americans residing in impoverished areas.

"In the Black community we essentially have four businesses. Drugs, prostitution, liquor stores and churches. And eighty percent of the churches aren't doing an effective job because they lack vision and are afraid to get involved in people's lives," says Campbell. "They do a good job with the people already in the church, but they need to get more involved in the community."

Campbell believes that Black churches should reach out a hand to single mothers in dire need of good child care; help find jobs for the unemployed; aid in community development; and help strengthen families.

With the help of his wife Brenda, Campbell recently began conducting marital enrichment seminars in churches in Texas. "If you break down the family, you've broken down society. Too many Christians are filing for divorce when we need to be setting the standards because we have the blueprint for how things should be."

Campbell is a tireless volunteer who has tutored grammar school and high school students, spoken to students during Black History Month and Dr. Martin Luther King, Jr. Day celebrations, and served as a group leader for Rites of Passage programs for young Black men.

If not for his family, Campbell could easily have chosen a less positive path in life. When he was only ten years old, his brother got involved with a gang and was shot. "The bullet hit his rib right in the front of his heart. If not for the bone there, his heart would not have been spared. To this day he still has epileptic seizures because of the gun shot," says Campbell.

After his brother was shot, Campbell's older sisters pulled together enough money to buy a building so that the family could live in a safer community. They moved into a primarily white neighborhood, where they were only the third Black family on the block. Some of their neighbors didn't exactly welcome them with open arms, but Campbell never allowed racism to keep him from accomplishing the things he wanted to accomplish.

"One white teacher told me I wasn't ever going to graduate. I distinctly remember going back and showing her when I made all A's and one B. Her negative input could have easily led to a self-fulling prophecy, but because of the positive role models I had early on, I learned to use racism as a positive influence that made me excel," states Campbell.

Fortunately, most of Campbell's teachers were more optimistic about his future. "There were a lot of instructors and other people who helped me along the way. I used to wonder what they got out of helping me. I discovered that my debt to them was to assist and help someone else."

Gwendolyn Young, executive director
Jefferson County Human Relations Department

By the time she entered the eighth grade, Gwendolyn Young understood the importance of seizing every opportunity that came her way. She took advantage of the array of self-improvement courses offered at the community center in Louisville Kentucky's Shepherd Square housing project, where tenants could learn everything from cooking and sewing to roller skating and math. She also joined the Explorer's Club, an organization run by a group of Jewish women interested in helping inner-city children.

"The women would come into the projects and take us to the theater, to fine malls and fine dining establishments. So even though I lived in a community where everyone was of the same socio-economic group, I knew that our environment was less desirable than others," says Young.

Young wanted to have a better life and there was no shortage of role models on hand to aid and encourage her. "My mother told me repeatedly that education was the key to progressing, and I had several positive teachers who were outstanding motivators. One teacher taught me typing as an extracurricular activity and helped me find baby-sitting jobs," Young recalls.

When a junior high school counselor told Young about the Lincoln School, a boarding school for talented children from financially disadvantaged families, Young eagerly signed up to take the entrance exam. Getting accepted into the Lincoln School was quite possibly a turning point in her life. For a girl from the projects with seven brothers and sisters, going to boarding school was a once in a lifetime opportunity.

"Teachers from Stanford and other prestigious schools taught at Lincoln, and Lincoln seniors were accepted at the best universities in the nation," says Young. Unfortunately, Lincoln was closed due to funding problems after Young's first year. Luckily she earned a scholarship to attend another private school in Louisville. When she learned of an even better school in Appleton, Wisconsin she went through an extensive testing process and gained admission there through the A Better Chance program. At the Loretta school in Appleton she lived in a home with seven gifted girls of diverse racial and cultural backgrounds. Young went on to Carleton College and to the University of Minnesota Law School.

The lion's share of Young's work as executive director of the Jefferson County Human Relations Department involves investigating charges of discrimination in the workplace. "One of the things I'm most proud of is passing the Minnesota and Kentucky bar exams, but I don't think I've made my greatest accomplishments yet. What I'd most like to do is to bring about positive changes for African-Americans in Louisville by getting more children to go to college and gain access to the employment opportunities that will raise their socio-economic level."

Howard L. Fuller, Ph.D.
Milwaukee School Superintendent
Milwaukee Public Schools

Howard Fuller has never stopped fighting. Years ago he participated in protest marches and organized groups of poor people in North Carolina to force landlords to treat tenants fairly. He was arrested in Cleveland for protesting segregation, but that only strengthened his dedication to the cause.

Today the battle is to reduce classroom sizes, to secure more alternative education options, to get good teachers and give them what they need to do their job right. Today the battle field is much different. He is no longer an impassioned young activist with nothing to lose. He is superintendent of Milwaukee Public Schools, a long way from the Hillside projects where he grew up in the 1950s.

"The higher you go, the more there is to lose, be it income or status," Fuller concedes. "But I've always been involved in controversy. The way I view it, I say what I have to say."

Fuller isn't surprised by his success. "I was fortunate in that many of the people who grew up in the projects with me are now doing positive things. The first Black deputy fire chief of Milwaukee was from Hillside, an editor for the Washington Post was from Hillside, a number of elected officials and quite a few principals in the Milwaukee School System grew up in Hillside," says Fuller, who earned a B.S. from Carroll College, an M.S.A. from Western Reserve University and a Ph.D. from Marquette University.

Fuller has lectured at such prestigious universities as Howard, Harvard, Cornell and Brown, and traveled internationally to speak at the University of Zambia and the University of Dar Es Salaam in Tanzania. He has taught at the University of Wisconsin, Marquette, Carroll College and the University of North Carolina.

"I've gotten a lot of breaks. I'm lucky in that people have taken an interest in me and helped me out, and certain positions have been vacant at a certain point and time," he says with modesty.

Fuller has not been lucky enough to avoid racism. "When you're African American, there is always a question of your competence. You're always put under a different microscope. But I've never allowed that to stop me from doing what I have to do."

Warrenton, Missouri Postmaster Bernice Brinker Wilkens has successfully managed to steadily progress in two careers and earn a college degree at the same time. Above Wilkens is pictured in her office at the Post Office. Below she is pictured (2nd from L) at her First Sergeant Class graduation.

Bernice Brinker Wilkens, postmaster
Warrenton, Missouri

Remember the tortoise and the hare?   Much like the tortoise,
Bernice Brinker Wilkens worked her way up slowly but surely from
the Vaughn public housing projects in St. Louis to her current
position as Postmaster for the U.S. Postal Service in Warrenton,
Missouri.

Her first postal job was as a manual distribution clerk at the
St. Louis Main Post Office in 1968. She transferred to the Weathers
Station Post Office in 1974. That same year she began a career in
the military. Not only has she advanced in both careers, but she
has had a positive impact where ever she worked. As she moved into
progressively more responsible positions at the post office, she
helped her employer cut down sick leave usage, cut back overtime
wages and improve layout in order to increase efficiency. After a
series of well-deserved promotions, she was sworn in as Warrenton
postmaster in March, 1991.

Wilkens' military career has been equally impressive. She
became a Staff Sergeant in 1977, a Sergeant First Class in 1980 and
a Master Sergeant in 1986. Last year the Secretary of the Army
awarded her The Army Commendation Medal for Meritorious Service
during her assignment as Chief Instructor of the Military
Occupational Specialty Division.

Although managing two careers was taxing, Wilkens decided
years ago that she also wanted to go to college. She came from a
family of nine children and, at one time, going to college would
have been virtually impossible. "Even if I was able to get money
for tuition, how would I have eaten?" she asks.

She worked full-time while she studied and it took her nine
years to earn an associate degree at Community State College in
East St. Louis and a bachelors in business and management at
National-Louis University. She graduated with honors.

Wilkens is keenly aware of the challenges facing public
housing residents. "When you grow up in public housing you don't
know how to go about entering the job market. These days that's
taught in many high schools, but when I was growing up kids in the
projects had no idea how to dress for success or how to learn about
a company in advance so that we could be prepared for an interview
and show a potential employer how our skills would help the company
reach its goals," says Wilkens. "I think often of all the people
who had a great impact on my life. People like my high school band
director who was always finding extra-curricular activities for us
to do. Kids in his class always wanted to do their best just in
case they ran into him. There were so many people who left a
positive impression on me and gave me a sense of direction as I was
developing."

Luckily for Wilkens, her 4th grade principal took a special
interest in her and helped her to acquire important job skills.
"My principal had a strong concern for Black children in poverty
areas and took me under her wings. In the summer she would allow
me to work for pay in her office. I would assist in reports and
mailings. She taught me office procedures and even took me with
her to Jefferson City once. I got to tour the Jefferson City
penitentiary. That had a lasting impact; I knew I never wanted to
go there!" laughs Wilkens.

The church also had a tremendous impact on Wilken's life. "I grew up in the Lutheran Church and remember going on church outings to the art museum, the mini opera and the zoo," says Wilkens. "Although we were poor, the church gave us an opportunity to give to those who were even less fortunate."

Wilkens would like to see successful African Americans who grew up in public housing form an organization to meet with people in the projects on a regular basis.

"A lot of times we are good at giving money. But we need to give time. Maybe we could teach young families how to plan healthier meals and better maintenance their households so they won't have to be dependent on someone else to do it for them. We could teach parents the importance of reading to their children so that, even if the parents don't want to leave the projects, their children can have a chance."

Captain Robert Walker
Birmingham, Alabama Police Department

Captain Robert Walker calls himself 'hard but fair'. During his 22 year career in the Birmingham Police Department he has put a lot of men behind bars. But he has also been instrumental in saving a lot of criminals from themselves.

"I understand why some people commit the crimes they commit because I come from the same background," says Walker, who grew up in the South Town projects in Birmingham. "I've been able to turn some people's lives around and now they are productive citizens. I had a friend who was selling narcotics for a while. I didn't have hard-core evidence, but rumors about him were spreading on the streets. I went to him to convince him to find another line of work. I carried him around and showed him some of the people on drugs and talked to him about how drugs are destroying our communities, how our men are losing their families and jobs because of drugs. Of course he already knew this, but I got him to acknowledge it," says Walker.

Some of Captain Walker's relatives still reside in South Town and he goes back frequently. "Some of the people I grew up with are still hanging out on the street corner with no ambition to do anything else. Others are still there but trying to move ahead."

"I used to go to church across the street from South Town. In church I was taught to respect other's rights and always try to help as opposed to trying to hurt other people," states Walker, who wanted to be a police officer for as long as he can remember.

Captain Walker has fond memories of South Town and of the school teachers who motivated him to succeed. "One teacher, Mr. Bell, used to say that we could achieve any goal we wanted to achieve and to not feel that we couldn't do things because we were from South Town instead of Round Mountain, a more elite area."

Captain Walker's mother worked at a dry cleaning establishment and always said that she was doing this kind of work so that her children would have more options. Walker is surprised about the number of parents who no longer seem concerned about their children's future. "Parents today need to be more attentive, and kids need to have something productive to do. I played a lot of sports, which kept me busy year 'round."

Although his title may impress some people, he says that nothing makes him more proud than his two sons.

Patricia Towns, attorney-at-law
Assistant vice-president and office manager
Chicago Title Insurance Company

Patricia Towns was among the handful of African American students who attended John F. Kennedy High School on Chicago's Southwest Side in the 1960s.

"I wanted to participate in sports but I couldn't because it wasn't safe for a Black person to stay at school after hours. I felt deprived and restricted. The atmosphere wasn't conducive to learning. But I felt that going to another school would be giving in," says Towns, who resided in LeClaire Courts, a housing project which was at that time the only Black community in the area.

"LeClaire Courts was such a small neighborhood and everybody knew each other. I felt perfectly safe within the community. Being surrounded by a larger white community and not being able to travel freely outside of the neighborhood bred a sense of belonging," recalls Towns.

The racism Towns encountered in high school had a lasting impact. Although she had an excellent academic record and yearned to become an attorney, one of her high school counselors suggested that she would make a good secretary and signed Towns up for typing courses.

"I recognize now the subtle form of racism. Her recommendations were meant to lower my self-esteem," says Towns. "They only served to make me angry and more determined."

When Towns graduated from high school she knew that she couldn't expect her parents to finance her college education. After all, she was one of nine children. But she was determined to find a way to get her degree. "I could have said 'no money!', thrown my hands up in the air and said 'Guess I can't go to college!'" she admits, but she had no intention of giving up so easily.

Fortunately she landed a job at Chicago Title Insurance Company, which had an excellent college reimbursement program. Ironically the first question they asked her during her job interview was "Can you type?" Thanks to the racist counselor who had steered Towns toward typing classes, she was able to get the job and complete her education. She worked full-time and took classes five nights a week. It took a total of ten years for her to finish her undergraduate and law degree at DePaul University.

Like many successful African Americans who came from low-income families, Towns knows that it is sometimes a struggle to move back and forth between two very different worlds. "In the white world we have to speak and conduct ourselves in one manner. When we return to the Black world we have to conform accordingly. Sometimes it's a challenge," she admits.

Occasionally brothers and sisters from the neighborhood jump to the conclusion that she is somehow less Black because she is a successful lawyer. But success has not dampened Towns' commitment to the Black community. "I feel a sense of responsibility for our race. The Jewish people have pulled together and they turn around and pull people up with them. That's why they've been able to have such an impact on society. We need to do the same," says Towns. "But you can't help anybody until you can help yourself."

Gerald Austin, Sr., founder and president
The Center for Urban Missions and New City Church

In 1987 Gerald Austin and his wife Gwendolyn took on a mission that many would call impossible. They set out to unify Christians of all races, denominations and socio-economic backgrounds in order to revitalize Birmingham's inner city. At a time when racism seems to be on the rise, Austin's Center for Urban Missions is bringing together people from all walks of life.

The center, which caters primarily to residents in the impoverished Metropolitan Gardens public housing community, has six dynamic ministries: a Metro Experience group for inner-city youth, a family care center, a choir made up of inner-city children, a Prime Time program for seniors and a program geared toward establishing churches in the inner-city.

Austin, who grew up in a public housing project in Collegeville, Alabama, believes that the majority of people trapped in poverty have the potential to escape. But handouts are not the answer. He doesn't believe in giving families a sack of groceries and sending them on their way. Instead, he inspires people spiritually and also responds to ongoing concerns such as job training, child rearing and drug abuse.

"We are committed to self-sufficiency," says Austin, an ordained Presbyterian minister who also founded the New City Church. Like the Center, the New City Church is made up of parishioners of all racial and cultural backgrounds.

"I think that churches have a tendency to become homogenous units, which as I look at the New Testament, the church was everything but homogenous. You saw Cretes, Greeks and Jews all part of worshipping communities. You saw people with wealth and those who were without share resources to bring about a greater sense of parity," says Austin.

But he is not naive to the realities of racism. When he was only 12 years old, a drunken white man walked up to Austin at a Farmer's Market and struck him in the head with a board, knocking him unconscious. Austin regained consciousness just in time to see his older brother confront the man. Soon the police arrived and they made an arrest. But they didn't arrest the man. They arrested Austin's brother.

Despite this injustice, Austin's mother taught her nine children to "never judge a person based solely on the color of his skin". Austin took this philosophy to heart. But his ability to accept and get along with all races almost served as his undoing during his high school years.

"I got involved in selling drugs, and operated as a middle man between whites and blacks. At that time, whites had drugs our community had never seen. Even though I knew it to be wrong, completely contrary to everything my mother taught me, I took advantage of my position and became deeply involved in a dangerous lifestyle," Austin says.

After high school Austin moved to Dallas to escape the negative life he had created for himself. He went to Debry Institute of Technology, earned a degree in electronics and found a good job. But he slowly slipped back into a negative lifestyle.

In 1974, a spiritual awakening inspired by a Christian insurance salesman led Austin back on the right track. He returned to Birmingham the next year. There he met his wife Gwendolyn, who had just started a Bible study class at Jacksonville State University. They shared the same spiritual beliefs and the same concern for the growing underclass. They began working with inner-city children and, after their marriage, they began a Bible study class at a downtown YMCA.

As their commitment to the city grew, it was inevitable that Austin would leave his position as a field engineer for General Electric Medical Systems and dedicate his life to the cause they embraced.

The Austins have six children of their own, but they are like second parents to countless children in Birmingham's poorest communities.

Lavette Burnette, honor student
Louisville, Kentucky

Sixteen-year-old Lavette Burnette cringes whenever anyone says she doesn't act like a girl from the projects.

"When people ask me where I'm from and I say I live in Beecher Terrace, sometimes they look shocked. A lot of people assume that people in the projects don't do anything right, so I like to prove them wrong," exclaims Burnette, an honor student and cheerleader at Central High School in Louisville.

"I think it's comical how people assume that students from the projects can't be as ambitious as any other students. It's so ignorant. Sometimes it makes me mad, but you can't be mad at ignorance," reasons Burnette, who has maintained a perfect attendance record throughout her three years at Central.

Unfortunately, many teens in Burnette's community have been convinced that they will never be successful. "I hear a lot of parents say 'you so stupid, you gon't be here all your life. You gon't be livin' in the bricks all your life.' So kids figure 'I ain't gettin' out of here so why bother with homework?'" says Burnette. "I know kids who did good in elementary school but pathetic in middle school and high school. A lot of them started hanging out with the wrong crowd. And if you're around negative people you will be negative. Some kids don't even want to carry books to school because that's not *hype*."

"People here don't believe me when I say I'm going to college and getting out of here. They think everybody is going to stay here, but I know a lot of people who got scholarships from here," adds Burnette.

Although many young people in Beecher Terrace have gotten involved with gangs and drugs, Burnette benefitted from the guidance of countless older residents who try to help youngsters in the community stay out of trouble. "In this neighborhood you see drugs all the time. You see people dealing them on the streets. But the older people look out for the kids. They say 'I'll tell your mother' or 'I'll tell your grandmother' if they see you doing wrong," Burnette says. "I can't say that I come from a close-knit family, but my mother does keep control of her kids and my grandmother is always around."

Burnette's high school principal, her cheerleading coach, her best friend's mother and members of her church have also been a source of support and encouragement. She says that joining the Joshua Missionary Baptist Church in 1987 gave her a sense of belonging. "It's a family church where you can really feel the hospitality. In fact, the church is helping to send me to Canada to tour African American sites. Another thing that helped me is that there are two community centers in the area. They help because I can go there and play games instead of being out on the streets," Burnette says.

In her sophomore year Burnette was nominated to attend the Hugh O'Brien leadership seminar, where students from around the country gathered for a weekend-long workshop. The seminar got her thinking more about how she could one day make a difference. Although she "can't wait" to get out of the projects, Burnette

hopes to one day be in a position to help her neighbors improve
their lives.

What will she tell kids when she returns to Beecher Terrace
years from now? "I'll tell kids that you should always accept help
from others. Don't let pride get in your way. I've also learned
that it doesn't matter where you live. Open your heart to the Lord
and he'll guide you where you want to go."

Keenen Ivory Wayans is pictured here on the set of Fox TV's hit comedy show *In Living Color*. Wayans is also an accomplished film writer and producer.

Keenen Ivory Wayans, executive producer, head writer and star
In Living Color.

When Keenen Ivory Wayans's hit comedy show *In Living Color* premiered in 1990, he suddenly emerged as one of Hollywood's most bankable young stars. But Wayans actually began laying the groundwork for his 'overnight success' years ago, when he was growing up in Manhattan's Fulton Public Housing Project. Inspired by Richard Pryor's television performances, Wayans decided at age six that he would be a comedian. He and his brother Damon honed their skills early by entertaining neighbors free of charge.

Wayans knew that he was a gifted comedian, but had no idea how to go about turning his hobby into a profession. At sixteen he began working 70 hours a week as a manager at McDonald's so that he could help support his nine siblings. Working full-time left little time for studying, but he still managed to win a scholarship to study engineering at Tuskegee. There he was exposed to a world that was totally different from the one he grew up in.

"I didn't realize how poor I was until I went to college. That was the first time I ran across Blacks from a privileged background. In the projects there was always somebody worse off than my family. There was a family downstairs that we gave our hand-me-downs to, and we were poor so you can imagine what a pair of shoes looked like by the time we gave them away," Wayans laughs.

"I was the first and only one of my friends to go to college and whenever I went back home they would ask me questions like someone in jail would ask. They'd ask 'What's it like in college?' 'What do you do?'" Wayans recalls. "The irony of the projects is that they look like cell blocks and they are mental cell blocks that keep people imprisoned. A lot of kids I grew up with got their own apartments in the projects."

But Wayans has no regrets about growing up in public housing. In fact, he suspects that living in poverty gave him the motivation he needed to succeed. "The projects are a great place to dream because when you're at rock bottom there's no place to go but up. In the projects everything was a miracle. Any happy moment was special. Christmas was like magic. Everybody in the projects felt that way. On New Year's everybody used to hang out their windows at midnight and bang pots and pans together. There was a lot of simplicity. A lot of family values. Everybody knew each other and I think that still holds true today. From an outsider's point of view the projects are worse than they are to people living there. In your own neighborhood you feel safe because you grow up with the future hoodlums," Wayans says tongue-in-cheek.

At Tuskegee Wayans learned 'stand-up' comedy by telling students stories about New York. In his senior year a friend saw him performing on campus and told him about New York's Improv comedy club. "I had to go all the way to Tuskegee to find out about the Improv which was located half a mile from my house," Wayans muses.

He quit college and began performing in New York comedy clubs in 1980. Later that year he moved to Los Angeles to pursue a career in movies and television. Although Wayans had no trouble finding work in comedy clubs, he quickly discovered that there were few good roles available for Black actors interested in film and television. Luckily he was accustomed to poverty and knew how to get by when cash was tight. "If you're a child from an environment like the projects, when you get into a softer environment it's easy. I got by on $2 a day in L.A. I knew how to make myself some canned corn and fish sticks and make a meal of it."

Fortunately, Wayans's lean days were limited. Like Spike Lee, Oprah Winfrey, Eddie Murphy, Arsenio Hall, Bill Cosby and other African-American entertainers-turned-entrepreneurs, Wayans was not content to sit back and wait for Hollywood to throw a few crumbs in his direction. Instead, he and Robert Townsend wrote and starred in *Hollywood Shuffle*, a parody of what Black actors go through trying to get work in Hollywood. They didn't have enough money to do an entire film so they did it piece by piece, using Townsend's money and credit cards to finance the project. After *Hollywood Shuffle* was released in 1986, Wayans co-wrote and co-produced *Eddie Murphy Raw*. In 1989 Wayans raised enough money to produce his own film, *I'm Gonna Git You Sucka*. The film, which cost $3 million to make, grossed $20 million.

Fox television executives were so impressed that they asked Wayans to create a weekly television program in which he could do anything he wanted. His creation, *In Living Color*, has been compared to everything from *Saturday Night Live* to *Laugh-In*. While the frequently risque program has kept censors hopping, the hilarious skits keep viewers tuning in. Not only have ratings been high, but the program's appeal to young viewers has helped it to pull in top advertising dollars.

Wayans is proud that his film and television projects have opened doors to other African Americans who might otherwise never have access to plum opportunities in front of and behind camera. He is especially excited about helping three of his talented siblings, Damon, Shawn and Kim, all of whom got their biggest breaks on *In Living Color*.

Although Wayans is enjoying his success in television and working on a new film titled *Blank Man*, he has found that the public frequently expects too much of Black celebrities. "I couldn't write a check big enough to solve all of the problems in the projects, but people think that because you're famous you can change something. But you're just a piece of sand that slipped through the cracks," Wayans admits. "The system is not set up for us to come up out of poverty. Yet people think that you have the solution if you made it out."

When Wayans visits Fulton he refuses to dole out advice unless someone specifically asks for it. "There's a thin line between passing out wisdom and being obnoxious," he states. "Besides, their perception is not that you had a plan to succeed but that you were just lucky. And to a certain extent you are lucky - lucky your plan worked."